taste

First U.S. edition published 1985 by Barron's Educational Series, Inc.

All inquiries should be addressed to:
Barron's Educational Series, Inc.
250 Wireless Boulevard
Hauppage, New York 11788

ISBN-13: 978-0-8120-3566-7
ISBN-10: 0-8120-3566-6

Library of Congress Catalog Card No. 84-28208

Library of Congress Cataloging in Publication Data

Parramón, José María
     The fives senses—taste.

     Translation of: Los cinco sentidos—el gusto.
     Summary: A short scientific explanation of our sense
of taste.
     1. Taste—Juvenile literature. [1. Taste   2. Senses
and sensation]   I. Puig, J.J.   II. Rius, María, ill.
III. Title.
QP456.P2713   1985   612'.87   84-28208
ISBN 0-8120-3566-6

Date of Manufacture: May 2018
Manufactured by: (Sagrafic S.L. / Barcelona / Spain)
Printed in Spain

the five senses

taste

María Rius

J. M. Parramón   J. J. Puig

BARRON'S

This tastes good to me!

But this tastes terrible!

Pastries taste good to me.

So does chocolate.

Oranges are delicious.

And milk is yummy!

Honey is very sweet…

...but lemons are very sour!

Sea water is salty.

Garlic and onions have a strong taste.

But what does water taste like?
Like nothing at all.

And what does meat taste like?
Like meat, of course.

The way you tell how something tastes
is with your TONGUE.

TASTE

Your *tongue* carries messages about what you eat to your brain. Your whole tongue is covered with little bumps called *taste buds.* There are different taste buds for each of four different types of tastes. That's right. Your tongue can really only taste four different flavors.

The front of your tongue is for *sweet* tastes like sugar. The sides of your tongue taste *sour* tastes like lemons, or vinegar. The back of your tongue tastes *bitter* things like grapefruit peel. You can taste *salty* things all over your tongue. The little nerve endings inside each taste bud carry the message to your brain and tell it what kind of thing you are eating. You can try all these different tastes on the different parts of your tongue and see what happens.

The *saliva* in your mouth helps you taste things, too. Your saliva mixes with the food you eat and carries the flavors to all the parts of your tongue. Food also tastes better if it isn't too hot or too cold.

But your tongue isn't the only part of tasting. Smelling is a very important part of tasting, too. Think about how things taste when you have a cold. When your nose is all stuffed up, you can hardly taste anything at all. If you close your eyes and hold your nose, you won't be able to tell the difference between a piece of pear and a piece of potato.

You might wish that you could only taste sweet things, but it's good to be able to taste everything. That way, if something doesn't taste too good, your brain can decide whether or not it's a good idea for you to keep on eating it.

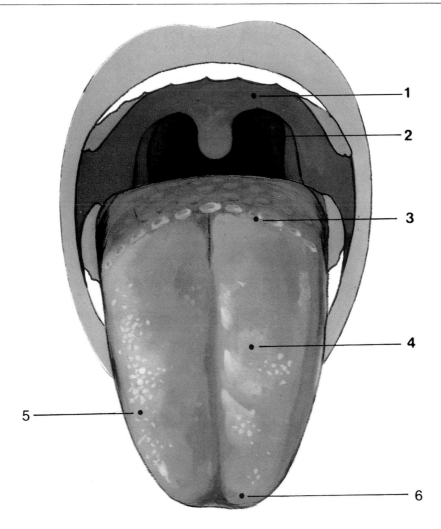

THE TONGUE

_____

1 Palate
2 Throat
3 Taste buds for bitter tastes
4 and 5 Taste buds for sour things
6 Taste buds for sweet things